THE MARKET TOWNS OF
LEICESTERSHIRE
& RUTLAND

The Market Place, Leicester, 1840. The open area of this ancient town could have held markets during the Roman occupation and certainly for over one thousand years. Today this site is more enclosed than depicted in this engraving, published in the early Victorian period. The Victorian architects have much to answer for; they organised the demolition of much of ancient Leicester. The 'Exchange', centre left, was built in 1748, originally the site of the magistrates' court and cells for prisoners. The 'Exchange' was demolished and the present Corn Exchange was built on the existing site in 1850, to a design by William Flint. One of the early markets, the Saturday market, was transferred to this open place in the medieval period, followed by the Wednesday market. Today a covered market operates from Monday to Saturday; the sale of corn and cheese no longer takes place at the 'Exchange'.

THE MARKET TOWNS OF
LEICESTERSHIRE
& RUTLAND

TREVOR HICKMAN

SUTTON PUBLISHING

Sutton Publishing Limited
Phoenix Mill · Thrupp · Stroud
Gloucestershire · GL5 2BU

First published 2005

Half-title page engraving: The Castle at Ashby
de la Zouch, 1832.
Title page engraving: The West Bridge at
Leicester, 1811.

British Library Cataloguing in Publication Data
A catalogue record for this book is available from the
British Library.

ISBN 0-7509-4137-5

Typeset in 10.5/13.5 pt Photina.
Typesetting and origination by
Sutton Publishing Limited.
Printed and bound in England by
J.H. Haynes & Co. Ltd, Sparkford.

By the same author
Around Melton Mowbray in Old Photographs
Melton Mowbray in Old Photographs
East of Leicester in Old Photographs
The Melton Mowbray Album
The Vale of Belvoir in Old Photographs
The History of the Melton Mowbray Pork Pie
The History of Stilton Cheese
Melton Mowbray to Oakham
Around Rutland in Old Photographs
Leicestershire Memories
The Best of East Leicestershire & Rutland
The Best of Leicester
The Best of Leicestershire
Battlefields of Leicestershire

The Market Place, Leicester *c.* 1900.

CONTENTS

Midland railway station, Leicester, *c.* 1900.

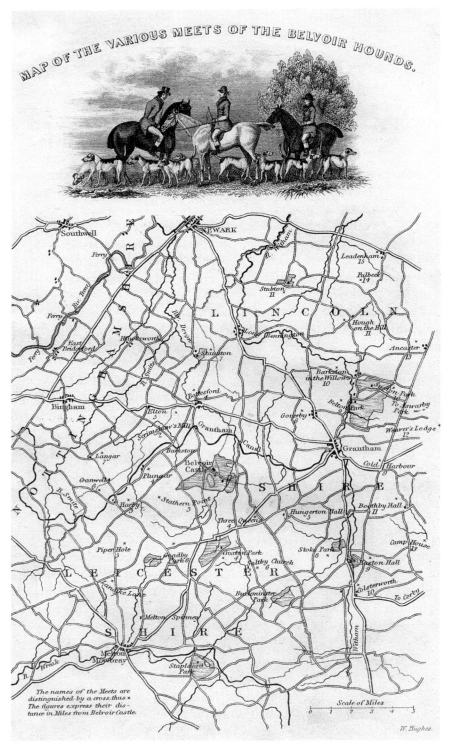

Published in 1847, this map shows the villages north of Melton Mowbray. Detailing the counties of Nottinghamshire, Leicestershire and Lincolnshire, it covers the area of countryside that was hunted by the Belvoir Hounds. It was printed from an engraving by W. Hughes.

INTRODUCTION

In this book are featured nine market towns: seven in Leicestershire, including Leicester, and two in Rutland. It is a personal collection of old and modern photographs with some drawings.

Ashby de la Zouch is steeped in history and has a fine ruined castle, which is controlled by English Heritage, with limited access. A small museum is well run by local volunteers, and there is a good selection of small shops throughout the town, with compact courtyard units. The parish church of St Helen is a fine structure and contains some excellent monuments carved from stone and wood. The Hastings family tombs stand well, and commemorate the famous family who resided at the nearby castle.

Loughborough is an industrial town with a fine university. Unquestionably the authorities have attempted to record their historic past and also to keep pace with modern developments. The street market has been maintained; the right to hold a market was granted to Lord Beaumont during the reign of Edward II (1307–27). One day is not sufficient to visit the historic features, shopping areas and market. The tourist information centre can provide visitors with an itinerary of places to visit.

Melton Mowbray is a traditional market town with a weekly cattle market, as well as the street market held every Tuesday, and is the only Leicestershire town with a market recorded in the Domesday Book. Numerous structural alterations have been made throughout the town. The town is the home of the famous Melton Mowbray pork pie and the centre for the equally famous Stilton cheese. The Carnegie Museum has excellent displays featuring these two famous products and also fox hunting.

Leicester is an interesting city which prior to 1919 was the county town, with large cattle and street markets. All the illustrations and photographs included here pre-date 1919. A considerable amount of Leicester has been lost, especially during the Victorian period and on into the twentieth century. All visitors are advised to visit the tourist information centre on Every Street, opposite the Town Hall. Most of the historic sites worth visiting are within walking distance of the centre of the city, particularly the Guildhall, museums and the excellent churches.

Hinckley's traditional street market takes place on a Monday, while on every third Thursday in the month a farmers' market is held in the Market Place, retailing quality local produce. There is an interesting shopping complex and the parish church of St Mary's is well worth visiting to view the memorials. Hinckley and District Museum stands on Lower Bond Street.

Lutterworth, a small market town with a traditional street market held every Thursday, is noted for the church reformer John Wycliffe, *c.* 1320–84, and Sir Frank Whittle, who developed the first jet engine for aircraft at a workshop in this town, 1936–41.

Market Harborough is sited on the River Welland, with a variety of shops scattered around the market square and in the side roads. Dominated by the splendid church of St Dionysus, the town has a very interesting museum in the Symington Corset Factory; the entrance is on Fox Yard. An occasional farmers' market is held in the square and there is a traditional market in the Market Hall, opened in 1993.

Oakham, the county town of Rutland, is fortunate in that considerable effort has been made to maintain its traditional character. A street market is held every Wednesday, with occasional farmers' markets. The church of All Saints stands near the site of a Norman castle; all that remains of this castle is a banqueting hall. Rutland County Museum is situated on Catmose Street and specialises in farming and rural history.

Uppingham is a market town with Uppingham School as a main feature, founded by Archdeacon Johnson in 1584, who also founded Oakham School. The historic town market is held on every Friday. Fine shops are laid out around the town centre, with particular emphasis on art galleries and bookshops.

Trevor Hickman

Thomas Badeslade's map of Leicestershire engraved by William Henry Toms and published on 29 September 1742. Badeslade drew this map to illustrate the market towns in the county. Organised markets were essential to ensure that a stable income existed for all those people living off the land, providing goods and produce for sale and barter. Most of the traditional markets were awarded by royal charters in the medieval period. The market days granted were: Leicester, Saturday; Ashby de la Zouch, Saturday; Market Harborough, Tuesday; Hinckley, Monday; Loughborough, Thursday; Lutterworth, Thursday; Melton Mowbray, Tuesday.

1

Ashby de la Zouch

In 1777 John Prior published his famous map of Leicestershire. He was master of Ashby de la Zouch Grammar School and lived and worked in the town. This is a detail from his map. All of the town is situated north of the castle; much has been written about Hastings Castle, built near the town. Clearly it is indicated as a ruin on this map; the position of the castle indicates how it withstood the months of attack and siege during the English Civil War. Cannon fire was directed from the south and easily repelled. According to the surviving records cannon were not aimed into or from the town, to avoid damaging the church of St Helen. Today the remains of the castle are completely surrounded by houses and business buildings.

As a market town Ashby de la Zouch contains some fine shops and a fair selection of public houses. The street market founded in 1210 no longer exists. Courtyard shops have been created, offering a wide range of produce and antiques.

Ashby de la Zouch Castle; an engraving of a drawing by W. Carter, published in May 1813.

The castle and chapel with the beautifully laid-out gardens, 1905.

Manor House and Ashby de la Zouch Castle *c.* 1910. For further information consult pp. 116–24 in *Battlefields of Leicestershire* (Sutton, 2004).

Mount Walk with the castle at Ashby-de-la-Zouch, 1908.

St Helen's parish church and the ruins of the castle, viewed from the road leading from Prior Park, *c*. 1910.

St Helen's church, 1928. The vicar at this time was the Revd Basil Charles Floyd Andrews.

The memorial to Edith, Countess of Loudoun, erected on the intersection of Bath Street and Station Street in 1878–9. Designed by Sir George Gilbert Scott RA, featured on the sides of this memorial are shields and arms of the Hastings family.

A photograph taken in 1912 of the Bath Building at Ashby-de-la-Zouch. Built from freestone in a Grecian Doric style, it was demolished in the 1960s.

May Day, with children dancing around the Maypole in the grounds in front of the building featured above, possibly in 1912.

Bath Street, with the Loudoun memorial, 1905. It features Fosters, Browns and Farmers, retailers, with a tram passing the memorial on its way to the station.

Charles Hussey Ltd, newsagent, stationer and tobacconist, next to the Bull's Head public house, before the Second World War.

Hill Street, Ashby de la Zouch, before the First World War.

The Roman Catholic church of Our Lady of Lourdes was founded by the 5th Duke of Norfolk. It was built on Station Road and completed in 1915; this is a contemporary photograph.

Two photographs of the same view of Market Street (top end): above *c.* 1910, below *c.* 1906. On the right stand two public houses, the King's Head and the George. Interestingly in both pictures a number of people have posed for the photographer.

Two views of Market Street. The photograph above was taken in about 1905 with a plough on display in the foreground; the photograph below dates from the First World War.

Market Street (lower end), *c.* 1910. There is a fine display of garden rollers in front of Holder's retailers.

Market Street, possibly a few years earlier than the photograph above, from a different angle. It looks as if the Saturday market has just been cleared away, with wicker baskets still stacked on the highway.

A flour bag that was used to convey flour and provisions from Hackett's Mill. Long since demolished, it was on the site of Hackett Close, off Smisby Road.

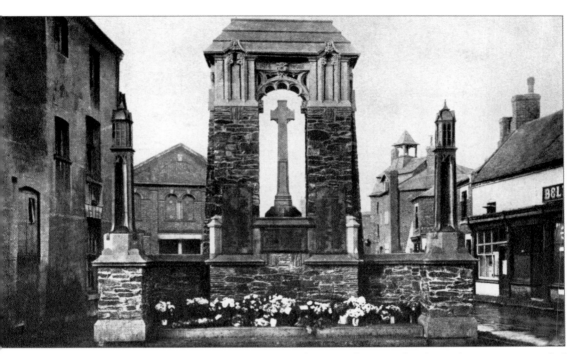

The war memorial that was erected on Market Street. This is a photograph taken when it was unveiled by Sir Joseph and Lady Hood on 8 June 1922, to record the men of Ashby de la Zouch who were killed in the First World War.

Market Street, with the Queen's Head public house on the right, June 2004.

Jo Humberston stands in front of the entrance to Ashby de la Zouch Market Hall, built in 1856. The splendid display of produce and flowers on the pavement shows that the street market is very much alive! This photograph was taken in June 2004.

Ashby Antiques in the courtyard situated on the west side of the Market Hall, along with other interesting shops, June 2004.

2

Loughborough

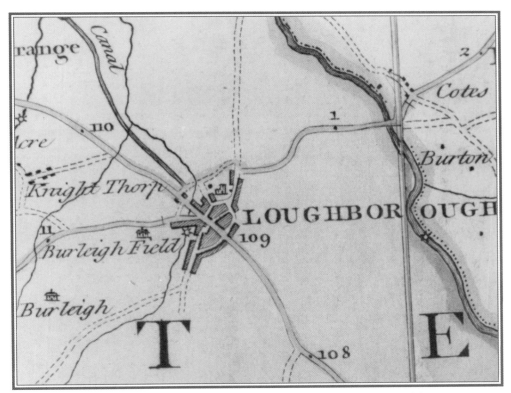

Part of John Prior's map of 1777, indicating Loughborough. The second largest town in the county after Leicester, it is an industrial town well aware of its past and records its history very well. Over the centuries the chief industries have been the knitting and weaving of hosiery, engineering, iron and brass machine works, a bell foundry, brick works and trade carried by canal, railway and road.

A record of Loughborough's history is well represented by the museum in Queen's Park, the Carillon nearby with its excellent displays and the Bell Foundry in Freehold Street. Unquestionably the Great Central Railway is well worth a one-day visit to examine the restoration of numerous steam engines. If you have enough time enjoy an evening meal while travelling by steam train through some lovely countryside.

Two engravings of All Saints' Church, north and south views, drawn by J. Pridden and engraved by J. Cook in June 1799. A thirteenth-century building, it has been considerably altered over many centuries. It is constructed in the Decorated and Perpendicular styles and is well worth visiting to examine the interior and view the record of the past.

The Rectory, Loughborough. This engraving was drawn by Langmate and published in 1794.

The Carillon in Queen's Park. This war memorial was completed in 1923 and it is seen here in a contemporary photograph. The tower is 150ft high with a total of 138 steps, and there are 47 bells. Three floors are laid out as small individual museums, displaying relics of the two world wars. This museum and memorial is maintained by enthusiastic volunteers.

Two images of Leicester Road, Loughborough, *c*. 1905. The photograph above was taken in the summer; on the right is the Royal Oak Hotel. In the photograph below the photographer stands opposite this hotel, in early spring.

Forest Road, Loughborough, *c.* 1930.

Church Gate, Loughborough, before the First World War.

The weir off the River Soar near Loughborough, 1910. This is part of the canal navigation.

The Grand Union Canal at Loughborough, *c.* 1920.

Loughborough Wharf and the Trent Junction on the Grand Union Canal, leading to Leicester, June 2004.

Constructing a display of bells at Taylor's Bell Foundry, June 2002.

A bell hanging in the Carillon, cast by Taylor's, dedicated to the memory of Walter Sellars and John Henry Lawton, killed in the First World War.

A steam-hauled train at the Great Central Railway, June 2002. For further information refer to p. 69 in *The Best of Leicestershire* (Sutton, 2003).

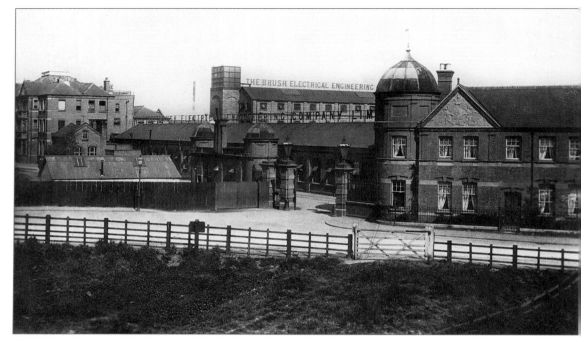

The Brush Electrical Engineering Works, Loughborough, *c.* 1920.

Queen's Park with the bandstand, 1905.

The lake in Queen's Park with the town's baths in the background, 1905.

'The Sock', demonstrating the importance of the hosiery industry to Loughborough, in the Market Place, June 2004.

Two views of the street market in the Market Place with the Lord Nelson public house in the centre background. The photograph above was taken shortly before the First World War, *c.* 1910. That below was taken during the First World War in 1915.

The Market Place, Loughborough, 1905.

The Market Place, 1912. Left to right are T & F Keightley, ironmongers; the Lord Nelson public house, and the Town Hall and Corn Exchange, built in 1855.

The Market Place, 1905. Compare this photograph with the one at the bottom of page 33.

The farmers' market on Devonshire Square with the Town Hall in the background, August 2002.

Two photographs of the street market in full operation in the Market Place, with the Town Hall in the background, June 2004.

The Market Place, Loughborough, June 2004. The market seen here maintains many hundreds of years of tradition in a fascinating town, a scene that is repeated in many historic photographs taken near the Town Hall since the turn of the twentieth century.

3

Melton Mowbray

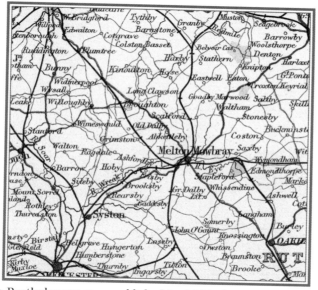

A section of a Bartholomew map published in 1920, featuring Melton Mowbray and the surrounding parishes. The market town developed on a crossroads connecting the East Midlands towns of Nottingham, Leicester, Grantham and Oakham. Markets have been held in the centre of this small town for over one thousand years, providing essential income for the inhabitants of both the town and surrounding villages. Without fox-hunting this town could not have developed; possibly today it would only be a very large village. Industry played an important part in the growth of the town, largely owing to Melton Mowbray pork pies. Their production was commercialised in the middle of the nineteenth century, and the factory became the biggest employer of workers making these pies until the outbreak of the First World War.

A good railway system was the key factor in the distribution of this famous pie. The Midland railway station on Burton Street was opened on 1 September 1846, and almost immediately pork pies were conveyed to London in specially constructed carriages. The London & North Eastern and Great Northern railway station was opened on 1 September 1879, to be closed on 7 December 1953. In the 1880s Thomas Nuttall built a large dairy to manufacture Stilton cheese next to this station, so enabling the delivery of his famous cheese throughout Great Britain.

Wilton House, 1837, later to be named Egerton Lodge, engraved by S. Lacey from a drawing by T. Allom. The home of the Earl and Countess of Wilton, they improved this lodge, commissioning the steps at the front of the house. The narrow bridge crossing the River Eye was built in 1822 and widened in the 1920s. St Mary's Church stands high in the background.

The River Eye in 1905, below Ankle Hill, next to the Midland railway station. Possibly this is where many of the bodies of soldiers killed in the English Civil War lay, turning the water red – ankle deep.

St Mary's Church, Melton Mowbray. This fine wood engraving was published in 1840 while Robert Fleetwood Croughton was vicar. Appointed in 1839, for nearly three years he caused considerable unrest among his parishioners. Many people attempted to raise funds to build a new church. In opposing his parishioners, he became insolvent and was arrested by an attorney from Peterborough and committed to the Queen's Bench Prison, spending some time there before being released.

The bandstand in the park at Melton Mowbray, 1910. In the background behind the bandstand Egerton Lodge is visible beyond the trees.

Leicester Road Bridge across the River Eye in 1905. Compare this photograph with the engraving drawn by T. Allom on page 38. If this illustration is accurate, considerable changes were made to this bridge after 1837.

The 'Toy Soldiers', the famous local band, demonstrating their skills in Melton Mowbray, 1924.

Croxton Park Races from a drawing reproduced as a wood engraving dated 6 April 1853. Sixteen years previously, on 6 April 1837, the Marquess of Waterford and a group of friends left the races for Melton Mowbray 'a little the worse for wear', having consumed too much fine wine.

Waterford and his friends arrived at the tollgate in Thorpe End, Melton Mowbray, in horse-drawn vehicles and on horseback at approximately 3am. The gates were locked for the night and the gatekeeper refused to open them. The drunken mob attempted to smash down the gates and attacked the gatekeeper; he attempted to defend himself with a pistol, but it misfired. At that time repairs were being undertaken on the gates and building, and large quantities of red paint were in store. Waterford and his gang stole the paint and commenced to 'coat in paint' the tollgate, keeper, and a policeman who had turned up because of the noise. This unruly mob then proceeded to charge down the main street 'painting the town red'. For further information see p. 18 in *Melton Mowbray to Oakham* (Sutton, 1998). This illustration was produced by Henry Alken to record the diabolical actions of a few so called gentlemen.

The Tourist Information Centre, 7 King Street, is housed in the remains of an early medieval-halled manor house. This building was almost certainly built in about 1330; dendrochronological dating of the crown post in the roof indicates this. It was built by John de Mowbray; the de Mowbrays were lords of the manor of Melton from the early twelfth century. Many changes have been made to the original structure, the most extensive during the Edwardian period when part of the front of the house was converted into a shop.

The Tourist Information Centre from St Mary's Way, which leads to the Bell Centre. When major restoration works were carried out it was decided that all phases of the numerous alterations that had taken place must be preserved. In this view from autumn 2004, the fourteenth-century roof on the right has been restored, as seen behind the Georgian extension, with the Edwardian shopfront, leading to King Street, retained. This street is named to commemorate Richard the Lionheart's visit to this manor house to thank the de Mowbrays for their help on his crusade to the Holy Land, and for raising some of the cash to pay for his release when he was held prisoner in Austria.

A postcard sent from Melton Mowbray on 30 July 1906 indicating 'What Melton Mowbray Pies are made of'. A Melton Mowbray pork pie is produced in a pastry case, filled with selected cuts of chopped pork mixed with selected herbs. A pastry lid is attached to the case, and when it is secured a hole made in the lid. It should be baked free standing in a hot oven. After it has cooled, gelatinous gravy is poured into the hole and allowed to set.

A Melton Mowbray pork pie, drawn in about 1920.

The Dickinson & Morris pork pie shop on Nottingham Street, *c.* 1930.

Thorpe Road, Melton Mowbray, *c.* 1910.

Burton Street, *c.* 1890. On the right is the Red Lion Inn with the hanging sign that was thrown into the Melton to Oakham Canal by the mob, led by the Marquess of Waterford, that 'painted the town red'.

Burton Street, Melton Mowbray, *c.* 1910. On the right is St Mary's Church. On the left is the sign indicating the entrance to the forge belonging to M. Bull, farrier for fox-hunters.

South Parade and Cheapside, leading to Nottingham Street and High Street, *c.* 1910.

South Parade, Melton Mowbray, 1908. On the left is Warner's, stationer, bookseller, printer and bookbinder and home to a library; Holgate's Leicester Boot Company; Manchester's furniture stores. Centre background is W. Barnes, hunt tailors, while on the right is Leonard Gill's motor garage.

A similar view to that above, with South Parade on the left and Cheapside on the right, 1910.

High Street, Melton Mowbray, *c.* 1910. In the centre background stands the Bell Hotel.

Nottingham Street, *c.* 1925. The Corn Exchange, built in 1854, is on the left. The Bass sign (right) indicates the premises of Skinner & Rook, wine and spirit merchant.

The Market Place, Melton Mowbray, 1905. On the left is the White Swan building, housing Pearce, tailor and clothier. Adcock and Pacey's public house The Corner Cupboard was next door. Rowell & Sons, boots and shoes for the hunting fraternity, is seen at centre, with W. Barnes, general drapers, dominating the market square.

Sherard Street, Melton Mowbray, 1903.

Park Road, Melton Mowbray, with a herd of cows being led from the cattle market, *c.* 1910.

The Carnegie Library on Thorpe End, Melton Mowbray, opened in 1904. It is illustrated here in a contemporary photograph.

The Tuesday market in the Market Place, its historic site, April 2004. Markets have been held in Melton Mowbray for over a thousand years and were recorded in the Domesday Book of 1085.

Twinlakes Park is an activity centre that has been created on farmland off Scalford Road. One of the many features in this park is the Falconry Centre. Richard James is holding Hal, a two-year-old male bald eagle. He escaped from his handler in May 2004 and terrorised the area around Market Harborough, seeking food. He was recaptured and this photograph was taken at Twinlakes in June 2004.

4

Leicester to 1919

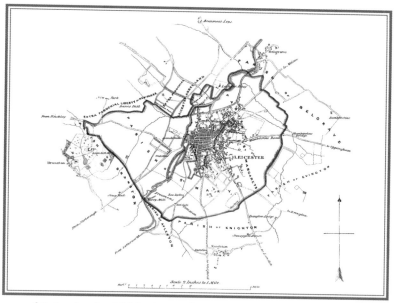

The town of Leicester in 1832, drawn by Lieutenant Robert Dawson of the Royal Engineers, who was employed by the Ordnance Survey. It shows the proposed extended boundary of the expanding town. On 28 June 1838 the coronation of Queen Victoria took place. The Victorian age saw much of ancient Leicester destroyed. On the title page is printed a reproduction of an engraving of the West Bridge in 1811, but nineteenth-century town planners did little to preserve the past and Victorian buildings have now become part of history, to be demolished in the twentieth and twenty-first centuries. The present-day planners of Leicester, especially the newcomers, should be aware of the old countryman's saying 'Lad! If you don't know where you have come from, you certainly don't know where you are going to!' In the following pages are a collection of nineteenth-century engravings and a selection of early twentieth-century photographs – a record of the past while Leicester was still a market town. In 1919 it was created a city and took on considerable national importance. A little of ancient Leicester still survives: visit the numerous museums, discuss the interesting features of Leicester at the Tourist Information Centre on Every Street, but above all support the market, one of the finest in Europe, and still held in the Market Place.

The town of Leicester viewed from the north in Abbey Park, 1882. St Margaret's Church and St Nicholas's Church can be seen to the right; to the left stands St Martin's Church.

A fine photograph of the Pavilion in Abbey Park, from 1904.

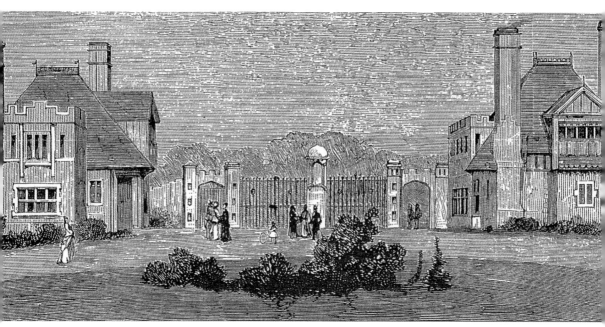

The entrance to Abbey Park. This ornamental gateway was opened by the Prince and Princess of Wales on 29 May 1882. The Prince of Wales became Edward VII when Queen Victoria died.

A photograph published in 1904, a similar view to that depicted in the wood-engraving above.

The Pavilion in Abbey Park on the banks of the River Soar in 1882.

The Japanese gardens in Abbey Park, Leicester, 1919.

Ruins at Cavendish House in Abbey Park, 1903. Charles I stayed in this house in 1645 when it was the Countess of Devon's home. Henry Hastings destroyed the building in June of that year. See p. 57 of *Battlefields of Leicestershire* (Sutton, 2004).

The entrance to Leicester Castle through the Turret Gateway, *c*. 1905. Many modern historians have renamed this Rupert's Gateway. Rupert's Tower stood on Bonners Lane, and was demolished when the road was widened. St Mary's tower stands high in the background.

Newarke Bridge, 1903, with St Mary's Church and the remains of Leicester Castle visible beyond the parapet.

Newarke Bridge. This photograph was published in 1905. Allotments, bowling green, extensive remains of the castle and motte are clearly visible, as is the site of Leicester Castle grounds. The canal towpath is on the left.

The courtyard of the Guildhall, from a wood engraving, 1882. The Guildhall was subject to a major restoration between 1922 and 1926, when the exterior plaster was removed.

The Mayor's Parlour in the Guildhall, *c.* 1910.

The Pavilion in Victoria Park, winter 1905. This magnificent building was damaged in a German bombing raid during the Second World War. Eventually it was demolished, even though funds were available and it could have been restored.

De Montfort Hall in 1919. This impressive hall was built in 1913 to a design by Shirley Harrison.

The Market Place, 1904. To the left is the Corn Exchange and in the centre of the market stalls stands the statue of the 8th Duke of Rutland. In the background is the drapery store of Turner & Co., nos 34, 36 and 38, next to the Silver Arcade.

Gallowtree Gate, c. 1910. Two Leicester Corporation trams run on the tramway, which was opened in 1904.

Market Street, Leicester, 1907.

F. Herington, draper,
milliner and ladies'
outfitters on Market
Street, 1907.

The Midland railway station on London Road, Leicester, 1903. The tramway had been laid but the passengers leaving the railway station are on a horse-drawn tram. Horse-drawn carriages were the main means of transport from this station before the electric trams came into full use in May 1904.

Granby Street, seen in a photograph taken just after the First World War had ended. The building on the left surmounted by a figure of Britannia is a hosiery factory owned by Moore Eady & Murcott Goode Ltd.

A postcard view of Hinckley Road, Leicester, posted on 15 December 1903, featuring an electric tram car. The opening ceremony for this new mode of transport took place on 18 May 1904 and as the track was completed it was brought into use; outlying streets came into service much earlier than the track in the centre of the town, especially around the clock tower. See pp. 18 and 19 in *The Best of Leicester* (Sutton, 2002).

Hinckley Road from the Fosse Way in Leicester, 1904.

St Stephens Road, Leicester, 1904. A splendid avenue of trees and no vehicles in sight, with the exception of the delivery barrow from Edward Allard & Co., grocer and provisions dealers of 112 Granby Street.

Narborough Road, Leicester, 1906.

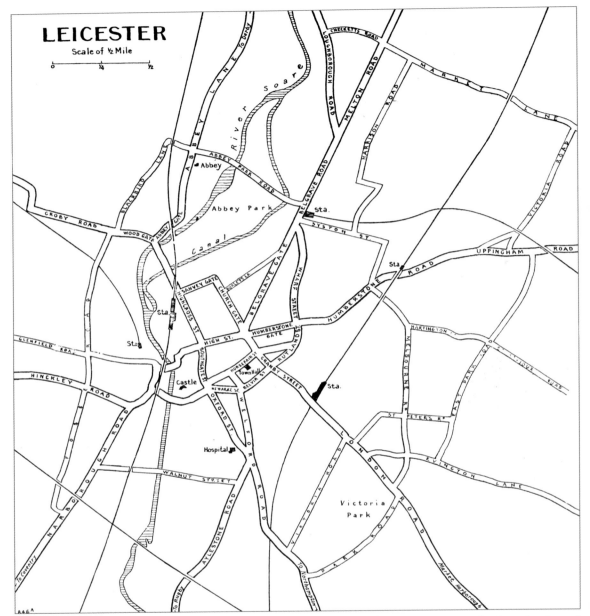

A plan of Leicester published in 1919. The main industries in the new city were hosiery, boots and shoes. The main roads are clearly indicated as well as the railway stations: the Midland on London Road, the Great Central at the junction of Highcross Street and Sanvey Gate and the Great Northern on Belgrave Road.

5

Hinckley

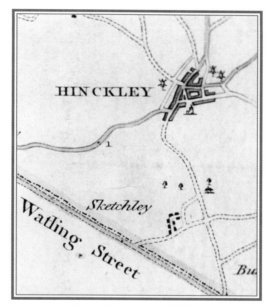

The town of Hinckley, as indicated on the 1777 map by John Prior, with three windmills shown around the town, which was situated near the famous Roman road of Watling Street. William Iliffe developed the stocking frame in 1640 and Hinckley became a centre for the hosiery trade. Trade was very important and the traditional market that operated on every Monday ensured that prosperity within this town was consolidated. During the nineteenth and early twentieth centuries boot and shoe manufacture and hosiery dominated the area. The dyeing and cleaning industry was important to the area too, and employed many local people. The well-known cleaning company, Sketchleys, was founded in Hinckley and named after the nearby village. There is a fine selection of small shops and an occasional farmers' market is held in the Market Place, normally on the third Thursday in every month.

The ancient history of Hinckley is difficult to research; the centre of the town is the site of a castle possibly built in about 1090 on the instructions of William the Conqueror. This castle withstood sieges and capture, but by 1460 it had been totally destroyed. In the castle grounds stands a fine memorial recording the names of those killed during the First and Second World Wars.

St Mary's Church, an early fourteenth-century building. This engraving was published in about 1790
The priory is on the left and the vicarage is on the right.

A photograph of the interior of St Mary's Church, 1910.

Argents Mead, a footpath leading from the castle site to St Mary's church, 1920s.

Argents Mead with the castle site in the background, May 2004.

Castle Street, with the Star Tea Co., and Bradley's (clothiers) on the left, 1906.

Castle Street with the traditional street market, May 2004. Redevelopment of the street has taken place piecemeal since the 1960s.

ation Road, Hinckley, 1905.

he war memorial erected on the castle site recorded the soldiers from Hinckley killed in the First World
Var. This photograph was taken in 1923 by John Baxter & Sons of 24 Castle Street.

London Road, Hinckley, 1914.

Spa Lane, Hinckley, *c.* 1920.

Burbage Road, Hinckley, 1906.

Hill Street, Hinckley, *c.* 1910.

Edmund Darwell Bailey and Reginald John Carter in a photograph taken by John Baxter & Sons before the First World War, in a greenhouse in Hinckley.

The General Post Office, Hinckley, *c.* 1910.

The Leicestershire Yeomanry 'D' Squadron sports day, at Hinckley, 11 July 1907.

This postcard is entitled 'Orpheus': it shows schoolgirls performing Greek dances at Hinckley, July 1923.

Hinckley Union Fete being opened by Mr Gustav Hamel, a pioneering Swedish aviator, centre, 20 July 1912.

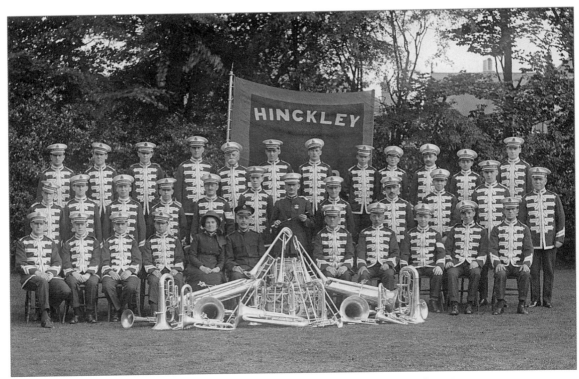

The Hinckley branch of the Salvation Army Brass Band based on Rugby Road, 1927.

Hinckley and District Museum on Lower Bond Street, May 2004. This museum contains many exhibits depicting the history surrounding Hinckley, with particular emphasis on the life of William Iliffe, who is believed to have introduced the stocking frame to the town.

The Roman Catholic Church and St Peter's Priory on Priory Row, Hinckley, 1912.

Stalls in the Market Place on market day, Hinckley, May 2004.

The Borough, Hinckley, May 2004. This stall is selling antiques on market day.

6

Lutterworth

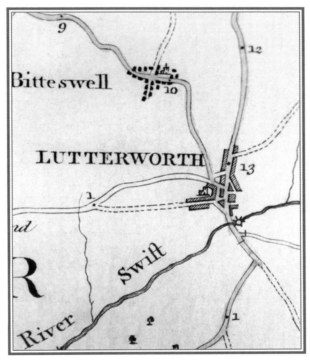

Lutterworth and the River Swift, from Prior's map of 1777. John Wycliffe, Lollard, church reformer and the first person to translate the Bible into English, died in Lutterworth on 30 December 1384. In 1428 the Pope ordered his bones to be exhumed and burnt, and his ashes thrown into the River Swift.

This is a splendid small market town. The weekly town market still takes place every Thursday with a farmers' street market on the third Friday in every month.

In 1938 Frank Whittle commenced work in a foundry on Leicester Road, developing the first jet engine for aircraft.

The church of St Mary and the Virgin is worth visiting to view the Wycliffe relics, as is the Town Museum situated in Wycliffe House on Gilmorton Road. This museum contains a good record of the town's past, including displays on the achievements of Sir Frank Whittle and John Wycliffe.

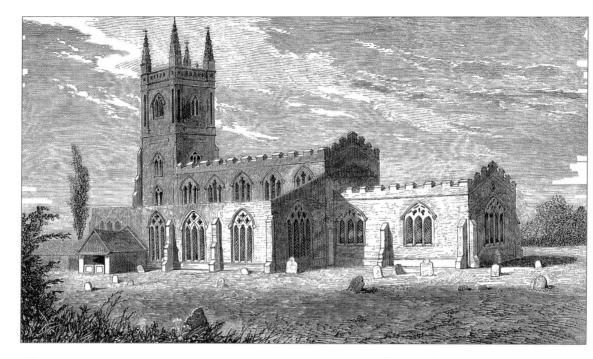

The church of St Mary the Virgin, a wood engraving produced in the 1850s. John Wycliffe was appointed rector in 1374, but without the support of John of Gaunt, Earl of Leicester, it is unlikely this church reformer would have survived to reach the age of sixty-four.

The 'kissing gate' at the entrance to the church of St Mary the Virgin, in 1904. This is a late thirteenth- to early fourteenth-century building.

The Greyhound public house opposite The Shambles with the town pump dominating the square, 1905.

Lutterworth Thursday market in front of The Shambles, 4 August 2003.

The church of St Mary the Virgin, 1906. On the left stands the Coach & Horses Inn, a sixteenth-century building.

Church Street, Lutterworth, with the Angel Inn on the right, *c.* 1910.

The market offices, with a noticeboard that lists the weekly and monthly markets. For a very small town the traditional markets are very well organised, ensuring that trade comes into Lutterworth from the surrounding district. The farmers' market is held on the third Friday in every month, organised by Lutterworth Town Estates.

A terracotta dog looks out over Market Street from a late Victorian doorway on the corner of Church Street, August 2003.

The traditional market in front of The Shambles, August 2003.

Collins the carriage builder with one of his completed carriages on display in front of his workshop, 1905. The Ram Inn, a half-timbered structure, is a few yards further down the road.

Bitteswell Road, Lutterworth, *c.* 1920.

The John Wycliffe memorial erected to celebrate Queen Victoria's Diamond Jubilee in 1897, with the church of St Mary the Virgin, where Wycliffe preached, in the background. This photograph was taken in 1906.

The Wycliffe memorial and the Methodist Church, built in 1905, on the junction of the Coventry and Bitteswell roads, c. 1925. See p. 138 in *The Best of Leicestershire* (Sutton, 2003).

The bridge across the River Swift in two photographs, one from each side of the river, *c.* 1920. Near this spot Wycliffe's ashes were thrown into the river in 1428.

The memorial to Sir Frank Whittle that stands on the junction of the Market Harborough to Lutterworth road, June 2004. Frank Whittle pioneered the design of the jet engine in 1936. Most of the design work was undertaken in a foundry on Leicester Road, Lutterworth, between 1938 and 1941. A Whittle jet-engined aeroplane, the Gloster E28/39, took off on 14 May 1941. This memorial records Whittle's achievements and this famous aircraft.

7

Market Harborough

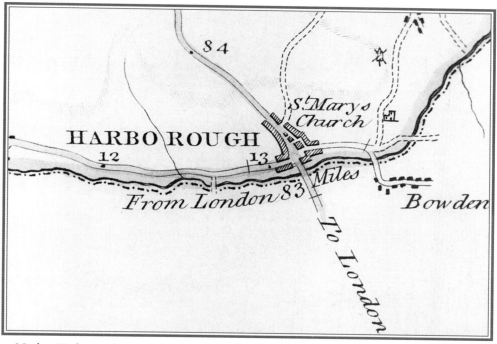

Market Harborough, as depicted on John Prior's map of 1777. The engraving illustrates the position of this small town in the county of Leicestershire, tucked into the south-east corner. London was 83 miles from Market Harborough on an important highway. A packhorse bridge and ford crossed the River Welland. Horse-drawn stagecoaches leaving north of London could just about reach this river crossing before a change of horses had to be made; exhausted horses were stabled at the many fine hostelries in the town. Such a scene is shown on the engraving of a change of horses, in front of the historic Grammar School, on page 88.

The Tuesday market generated considerable income in the market square. The sale of sheep and cattle ensured that the town was supported with traders from a large area of the Midlands. Today the market has been established in the Market Hall, which opened in 1993. The history of this town and the surrounding villages is well recorded in the Town Museum, the entrance to which is on Fox Yard.

Market Harborough, 1837, engraved by S. Lacey from a drawing by T. Allom. A change of horses is being made from the London to Manchester coach, refreshments are being purchased and baggage is being loaded into the boot. The Three Swans hotel is on the left, St Dionysus' Church in the centre and the Grammar School is on the right.

The old Grammar School standing in front of St Dionysus' Church, in 1905.

This is an unusual view from the east of the church and the old Grammar School, *c.* 1910. In this courtyard is a carrier cart, with a latrine at the rear of the school.

The Free Grammar School, founded by Robert Smyth in 1614 and seen here in June 2004. This spectacular building dominates the town.

Two photographs taken from the town square, possibly twelve months apart, *c.* 1905. The church dominates the horizon. Emerson's and Hilton's are trading off the square. During the autumn 'Hilton's Autumn Boot Sale' was held.

A charming view of Leicester Road with the entrance to Bowden Lane on the right, *c.* 1905.

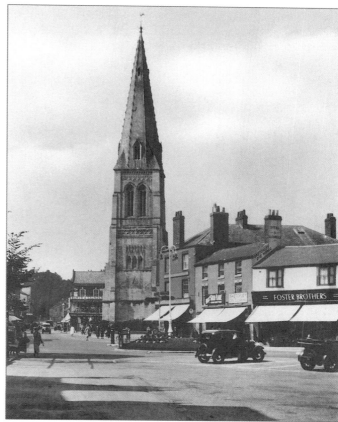

Compare this photograph from the 1920s with the photographs on the opposite page. Foster Brothers have taken over Emerson's shop and altered the roof.

Two views of the High Street, Market Harborough, *c.* 1905. It was a tranquil town at this time, as the stage-coach trade had collapsed and the age of the motor car had yet to arrive.

The River Welland at Market Harborough with a footbridge crossing the river, *c.* 1905. Visit the river bank today, and such views still exist.

Northampton Road, Market Harborough, with the Wesleyan Methodist Church on the left, *c.* 1905.

High Street, Market Harborough, with the Three Swans Hotel on the left, 1907.

An aerial view of Market Harborough, c. 1930. The house in the photograph at the top of page 91 can just be made out at the top left of this scene.

A street market still continues in the Market Square. In the two photographs the farmers' market is in full swing, June 2002.

Farmers' market, June 2002.

The Market Square, showing the
influence of modern development,
June 2004.

Entrance to St Mary's Place, Market Harborough, June 2004. In this courtyard there is access to some fine shops, including bookshops.

Entrance to the Market Hall, opened in 1993; this hall contains an excellent arrangement of shops, June 2004.

Sandra's Cheese Stall in the Market Hall, June 2004.

Harry Brown's butcher's stall in the Market Hall, June 2004.

The Union Wharf Canal at Market Harborough, June 2004. This canal basin was built in 1809; now it has now been converted into a twenty-first-century marina.

An arm of the Grand Union Canal, from Foxton Locks, leading to the Union Wharf Canal at Market Harborough, June 2004.

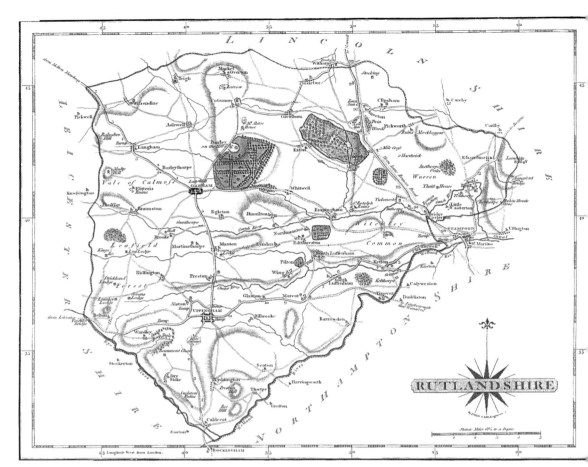

A map of 'Rutlandshire' engraved and published by John Cary, 1 September 1787. An outstanding cartographer, during the late eighteenth century he revolutionised the production, marketing and publishing of atlases. In 1794 the Postmaster-General commissioned Cary to survey the roads of Great Britain and in 1804 he was awarded a gold medal by the Royal Society of Arts.

This is a very small county as clearly indicated on this map; there are only two towns – Oakham, the county town, and Uppingham. 'Occa's *ham*' possibly refers to a Saxon landowner who did not survive the Norman Conquest. Anglo-Saxon queens owned the area around Oakham until the Ferrers family were granted the land by about 1130 by Henry I, who had married a Saxon girl in an attempt to unify England, after it had been gained by his father, William the Conqueror.

8

Oakham

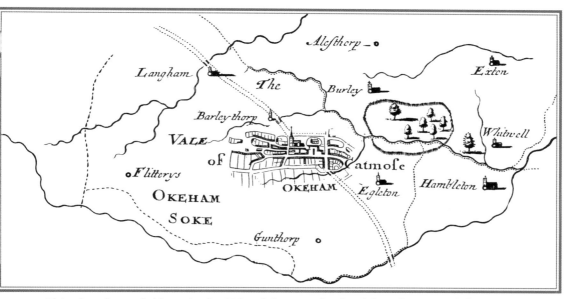

This plan shows Oakham in the Vale of Catmose, bordered by tributaries of the River Gwash, in the early eighteenth century. All Saints' Church dominates the town and the fortified manor house is featured. Oakham grew as a market town under the patronage of the Ferrers family, lords of the manor, who were granted the right to hold markets and fairs during the reign of Henry II, 1154–91. Archdeacon Johnson founded Oakham School in 1584; this fine public school has done much to maintain the historic character of this traditional market town. Interesting shops are scattered around the town in the streets off the market place. Rutland County Museum stands on Catmose Street, constructed in 1794 as a riding school for the Rutland Fencible Cavalry. It was converted to the county museum in 1969 and contains some fine permanent displays featuring agricultural equipment. Purpose-built rooms contain a farmhouse dairy that produces butter and cheese, a cooper workshop, a variety of shops and some excellent displays of archaeological discoveries. One part of the museum is devoted entirely to the military history of regiments connected with the county of Rutland.

Oakham Castle, *c.* 1920. Considered to be a 'castle' because of its location, it was a place of importance in the county town, where all laws would have been passed by the controlling lord. From the twelfth century this was the Ferrers family, headed by the Earl of Derby. It was not the main centre for these medieval lords; Oakham Castle was one of their 'outposts', built as a fortified manor house and defended with a walled moat. During the early years of the Norman Conquest possibly a motte and bailey defensive system was erected.

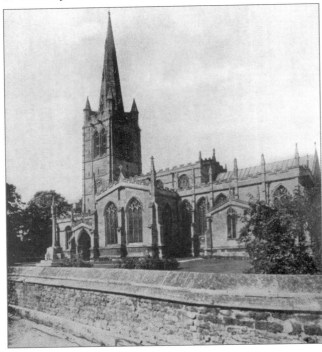

All Saints' Church from the south-east, 1934.

An engraving of the Norman hall, a fortified manor house, *c.* 1715. Considered to be a banqueting hall occasionally used by the Ferrers family, it was only lightly defended. In this illustration the defensive walls surrounded by a moat are still being maintained.

A selection of the famous horseshoes on display inside Oakham Castle. Custom demands 'that the first time any peer of this kingdom shall pass through the precincts of his Lordship, he shall forfeit as a homage a shoe from the horse whereon he rideth, unless he redeem it with money'. At the time of this photograph, *c.* 1910, the banqueting hall had been converted into a court of law.

The defensive walls of Oakham Castle viewed from the Burley Road car park, 2005.

The post mill that stood on Ashwell Road. This windmill would seem to have operated until the 1890s, with Joe Smith possibly the last person to grind corn in this mill. The photograph was taken before the First World War.

The 'Oakham Horse', *c.* 1930. Justin Littler MRCVS, veterinary surgeon, is stroking his cat next to the topiary horse. Justin 'trained' this horse on the hedge at Oakham House that stands on the junction of Station Road and Kilburn Road.

This postcard was sent from Oakham on 26 September 1910. There are six donkeys, the joke of the caption being that it was obviously sent by the seventh!

A sheep market being held in the Market Square in 1905 in front of G.E. Barnett's butcher's shop. The George Hotel is on the right.

Market Square with the George Hotel on the right, *c.* 1910. Before the First World War this hotel provided a garage with a car pit for servicing. To the left of the hotel is Pratt's stores, retailers of motor spirit.

A photograph taken in about 1915 of shops on Burley Road: Herbert Buttress, butcher, Thomas Clarke, baker and Thomas Walker, printer. It is interesting to note that the famous Melton Mowbray pork pies are displayed in the window on the left.

Wicker baskets being sold in the Market Square on market day, 2005.

The Whipper-in Hotel, formerly the George. The hotel's new name refers to fox-hunting, a traditional activity in this area of England (see pages 113 and 114).

The Butter Cross and stocks, Oakham, with F.W. Hart's grocer's shop in the background, *c.* 1905.

The town pump with the Butter Cross in the background, *c.* 1910.

The town pump, *c.* 1930.

The town pump with the market in full swing behind it, 2005.

Delivering bread on Northgate Street, Oakham, *c.* 1910.

High Street, Oakham, looking west with the Crown Hotel on the left, *c.* 1900. In the centre background stands Flore's House, an early fourteenth-century merchant's house.

High Street in the 1920s. Flore's House has been subjected to considerable alterations: part of it was demolished in a road-widening scheme, and some of the early sixteenth-century windows were lost forever.

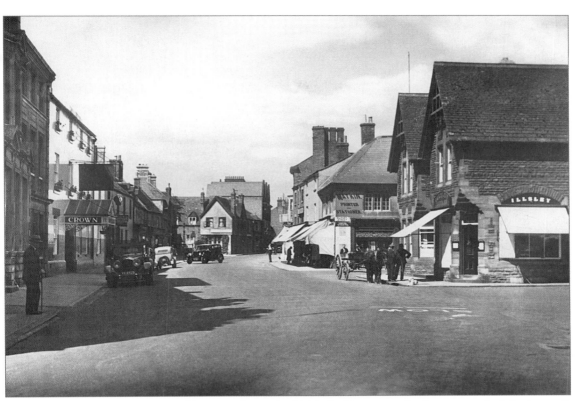

Two views of the High Street, Oakham, in the early 1930s looking towards the west end of the town. It was a typical market town before the outbreak of the Second World War; very little change has taken place when these two photographs are compared with the one at the top of page 110.

Two views of the High Street, Oakham, looking east, *c.* 1910. On the left is G.H. Thornton, general household engineer. In the centre background is Lenton, grocer and general provision merchant, and on the right is the Crown Hotel.

A recent advertisement for the Boxing Day hunt.

Fox-hounds and riders waiting for 'the off' at Cutts Close, Oakham, Monday 27 December 2004.

The Cottesmore Hunt, founded in 1666 and expanded in Rutland in 1695, meeting at Cutts Close, Oakham. Spectators are standing on the medieval embankments, the walls that defended the nearby manor house. The joint hunt master, Kim Smith, is about to speak briefly to the spectators about this traditional country sport.

'Come on, I am waiting for "the off".'

Two young riders waiting for the hunt to leave Cutts Close.

The Cottesmore Hunt leaving Cutts Close on their Boxing Day Meet, December 2004. They are passing the Odd House Tavern on their way to the first draw in Burley-on-the-Hill woods.

9

Uppingham

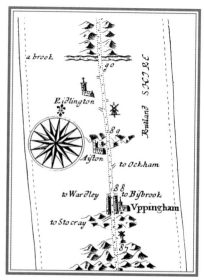

This is an extract from one of John Ogilby's maps published in his atlas of 1675. It indicates that Uppingham is a junction town on a post road, with London 88 miles away. These strip maps were produced to enable travellers to recognise the countryside through which they were travelling on horseback. Many of these atlases were damaged as the travellers removed the relevant pages and carried them in their pockets. This changed in 1720 when Emanuel Bowen published a pocket atlas, copying Ogilby's earlier maps. This was small enough to be carried in the pockets of the post boys travelling the length and breadth of England.

On this map is featured the windmill south of the town and the church of St Peter and St Paul. A church is recorded in Domesday Book. A Saxon settlement, there is reference to *Uppingas*-ham – people on a hill. Produce would have been sold during the Saxon period on such an important highway. The Friday market was first granted by Edward I in 1281. This market still flourishes, with a farmers' market and the annual Christmas fatstock show and sale held in the Market Square.

In 1584 Archdeacon Robert Johnson founded Uppingham School; originally this was a small grammar school. In 1853 the Revd Edward Thring was appointed headmaster, and for thirty-four years through his energies it developed into a flourishing public school. It was rebuilt in 1863. In the following pages are a number of photographs recording this very fine historic establishment.

The church of St Peter and St Paul, 1934. Built in the Perpendicular style, it contains a chancel, four bays with aisles, north and south porches and a western tower with spire. The church was altered and restored in the Victorian period, but the Jacobean pulpit was retained.

Uppingham School, the shrine to Thomas Becket and the headmaster's house, c. 1930.

Uppingham School War Memorial Hall, 1905.

Uppingham School War Memorial Hall, being opened by Field-Marshal Earl Roberts VC, KG, on 30 March 1905. By 1916 it was used as a concert hall and gymnasium.

Uppingham School, *c.* 1910.

Uppingham School XI, 1915: C. Whitehead, Captain; H.J. McKenzie; S.P.H. Smith; E.H. Tattersall; K.P. Bell;
R.S.G. Vigers; G. Robinson; F.A. Waldock; J.L. Horridge; S.R. Gresham; H.W.G. Craigmile.

School House, Uppingham, *c.* 1920.

The Old Schoolroom, Uppingham, *c.* 1920.

Uppingham School Hall, *c.* 1920.

Lower School, Uppingham, *c.* 1920.

Uppingham Auxiliary Hospital, *c.* 1915.

Uppingham station, 1907. It opened in 1894 on a branch line from the London & North Western Railway and was closed in 1964.

Church Hill, Uppingham, 1905. To the left stands the National School and the Uppingham Improvement Society building, demolished in 1974. In the background stand the tower and spire of St Peter and St Paul's Church.

Orange Street, Uppingham, 2005. Goldmarks is one of the leading provisional dealers in fine art in the United Kingdom. On this street it is worth visiting the collectors' shops that offer a fine selection of interesting items.

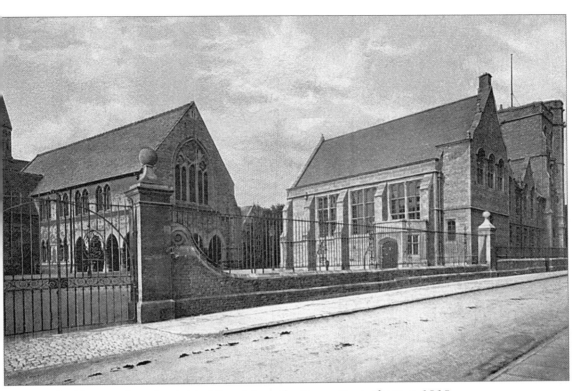

Victorian buildings and, to the right of the picture, the Tower, Uppingham, *c.* 1910.

The Market Place, Uppingham, *c.* 1930. The Vaults public house is in the background.

Uppingham fatstock show, Market Place, Wednesday 1 December 2004. This was the ninety-ninth Christmas fatstock show. Entries consisted of 29 cattle, 180 sheep and 31 pigs. This animal agricultural show is well known as being the only event of its kind in England, where stock is penned in temporary hurdles in a town market square.

The right to hold fairs and markets in the town of Uppingham was granted by Edward I in 1281. This gave the people of the town and surrounding villages the right to display and trade livestock and goods. In all the market towns featured in this book that have been granted the right to hold such markets, as illustrated above, Uppingham is the only town that maintains this historic heritage.

The Friday market in the Market Place, Uppingham, January 2005.

Market day with the Vaults in the background, 2005.

When visiting Uppingham take a stroll down High Street, westwards; there are some interesting shops, notably second-hand bookshops.

SELECT BIBLIOGRAPHY

Brownlow, J., *Melton Mowbray, Queen of the Shires*, 1980
Kelly's Directory of Leicestershire and Rutland, 1900, 1904, 1916, 1922, 1925
Butt, R.V.J., *Railway Stations*, 1995
Cavanagh, T., *Public Sculpture of Leicestershire & Rutland*, 2000
Fielding Johnson, T., *Glimpses of Ancient Leicester* (2nd edn), 1906
Pevsner, N., *Leicestershire and Rutland* (2nd edn), 1984
Pearson, M., *Me, My Morgan & The Midlands*, 2002
Hoskins, W.G., *Rutland: A Shell Guide*, 1963

ACKNOWLEDGEMENTS

In 1992 Sutton Publishing released the first book I had compiled for them; this is the fifteenth book I have written for these publishers. All these books have been concerned with local history and feature the counties of Leicestershire and Rutland. In researching the previous fourteen titles, to check the accuracy of my observations and comments, I visited all of the towns and nearly every village in the two counties. It was apparent to me and my publishers that a record of the traditional historic market towns I had visited was worth publishing. Jo and Don Humberston joined me when I revisited all of the market towns in Leicestershire. Keith Badcock was very helpful in supplying photographs and information when I visited the two towns in Rutland. The *Rutland Times* provided the photograph of the Uppingham fatstock show on pages 124 and 125; they retain the copyright. Many of the historic images in this book are out of copyright and I hold the originals in my collection, or the copyright belongs to me, the author. Once more I thank Jenny Weston for processing my manuscript for submission to my publishers.

INDEX OF LOCATIONS